EPISCOPAL HAIKU

The Church, Its Ways, and Its People, Seventeen Syllables at a Time

Sarah Goodyear and Ed Weissman

T0117745

Seabury Books

An imprint of Church Publishing Incorporated

NEW YORK

Library of Congress Cataloging-in-Publication Data

Goodyear, Sarah.
 Episcopal haiku / by Sarah Goodyear and Ed Weissman.
      p. cm.
 ISBN 978-1-59627-079-4 (pbk.)
 1. Christian life--Episcopal authors. I. Weissman, Ed. II.
Title.
BV4501.3.G6587 2007
283'.73--dc22

                                             2007030110

Church Publishing, Incorporated.
445 Fifth Avenue
New York, New York 10016

5 4 3 2 1

CONTENTS

INTRODUCTION

The haiku is a multilayered and complex poetic form originating in Japanese culture, characterized by a three-line construction and requiring deep contemplative thought from the reader. Don't worry, we only borrowed the form.

This collection aims to hold up a mirror to life as lived today among Episcopalians. Our perspective is humorous, although, as we reflect the mosaic that is the church, a somber note can be found here and there.

Read this book as you will. Our order need not be yours. Our points of view may very well not be yours.

As with the Book of Common Prayer, a most important word is "or."

The final word belongs to Good Queen Bess (quoted in Bobrick, *Wide as the Waters*).

"There is only one Jesus Christ.
The rest is a dispute over trifles."

BEING
EPISCOPALIAN

No fair looking when
you put your offering in
the collection plate.

The great litany:
saying it is like walking
the great labyrinth.

We'll cheer at the game,
but never at church. What would
people think of us?

Foot-washing seems strange to some. But they just love to get a pedicure.

Pyx, paten, psalter,
chasuble, reredos, alb:
ancient words, now ours.

At a new age church,
the liturgy seems quite strange.
It's rite twenty-five.

Episcopalians:
an elite reputation.
Most of us: not rich.

Let's count the clichés
about Episcopalians.
I can't count that high.

Half Jewish and half
Episcopalian means that
I can eat *and* drink.

Welcome to our church.
Let me show you our founders,
here in the churchyard.

Most parishes think
they're Congregationalists
with Bishop on top.

It is said, when two
Episcopalians gather
a fifth is present.

When on the vestry,
friends you've known for many years
suddenly go nuts.

The way you can tell
what rite any church uses:
pages edged in black.

At seminary
the age of the new students
gets closer to mine.

St. James Madison
is a New York church, not a
canonized POTUS.

Churches have nicknames.
Church of the Heavenly Rest
is Celestial Snooze.

Another nickname:
St. Mary the Virgin is
called Smoky Mary's.

Dear Reader, why don't you think up a nickname for your church and share it.

CHURCH LIFE—
SUNDAYS

Pews haven't been sold
for at least a century,
but this is my pew.

Do priests really see
God better with their backs to
the congregation?

If only cookies
could be as calorie-light
as some sermons are.

Slow sermon. Mind drifts
up to a window that lets
in green light, birdsong.

Seminarian's
sermon: Rookie swings for the
fences and connects.

Our hands try to hold
the Hymnal, prayer book, readings–
and they all fall down.

Handshakes at the peace:
some limp, some crushing, some damp.
God made all those hands.

We're passing the peace.
Passing and passing the peace.
It's the social hour.

Stand, sit, kneel, stand, kneel: it's quite a good workout for a Sunday morning.

Kneeling at the rail
you see the priest's scuffed shoes. It's
like peeking backstage.

Ever notice how
some priests gaze at your forehead,
never in your eyes?

Some chalice bearers
tip out a real glug of wine.
It makes me dizzy.

We sing the last hymn.
The candles are extinguished.
Okay to leave now?

The Church: historic,
but only because it's old.
Just faith happened here.

Ah, the coffee hour.
Certain people talk to me.
It feels like an hour!

A rainy Sunday
is the time to discover
the forgotten church.

Stones underfoot say IN MEMORY OF. With our shoes, we polish them.

KIDS

A little girl drops
her wafer in the wine. She's
soaking up God's grace.

See the junior choir,
like a row of pert sparrows
singing their hearts out.

The little ones ask
questions that would confound a
learned archbishop.

Who is that man and
what is he doing on that
cross? Mommy? *Mommy?*

They color in their
pictures of Jesus with care.
What are they learning?

When you're five, turning the other cheek is tough. For grown-ups, tougher still.

Squalling kids in the
last pews: far from the altar,
but closest to God.

Sunday school scuffle
breaks out: Who will be a lamb
and who an angel?

Only life prepares
Sunday school teachers for the
daunting task ahead.

Swallowing God is
Easier with two cookies
and a cup of juice.

Teachers, you'll learn this:
All children start their lives as
fundamentalists.

At the font: blessing,
sluicing water, cross of oil,
a baby's complaint.

Children wonder why
the bread at communion is
not like bread at home.

MUSIC

All God's instruments
have a liturgical role—
except the guitar.

The choir rehearses.
A soprano fails to curb
her inner diva.

The choir's away and
the rest of us suddenly
have lost our voices.

Some hymns wander from note to note, like Israelites lost in the desert.

Gilded organ pipes
promising a symphony—
but they're just for show.

Those who cannot sing
make sure ev'ryone knows it.
They sing the loudest.

Do we have to sing
all the verses of each hymn?
We're just a small church.

This "Christian music"
is a genre to itself.
But what about Bach?

CHURCH LIFE—
THE REST
OF THE WEEK

All this brass for the
glory of God: the very
Devil to polish.

Rector's popular.
He's always in great demand.
That means he'll move on.

To sell at the fair,
they bring junk that Jesus would
have trouble loving.

Monthly newsletter.
What's going on at the church.
Some said, some unsaid.

Blessing animals
is a joyous day at church.
Who has ugly pets?

At pot-luck dinners,
why do people keep bringing
food from the '50s?

No one ever sees
his own errors or mistakes
as well as others'.

Rehearsing readings,
folks fear they'll mispronounce names.
But who knows what's right?

Are outreach programs
an admission of failure
or of a new hope?

How many vestries
debate, debate, and debate.
And still can't decide?

A revelation:
some time in the last few years,
you joined the old guard.

A vestry of nine
often will be split at least
eighteen diff'rent ways.

The congregation,
at the annual meeting,
approves ev'rything.

Tourists like our church.
They look around the building
and donate a dime.

Our churches are in
the English style: grand, gloomy.
Inside, New World fizz.

SEASONS
AND HOLIDAYS

Advent calendars
really cannot compete with
displays at the mall.

Lessons and carols
is my favorite service.
Just once a year. Sigh.

Two feet of new snow
and here I am in our church.
I should be skiing.

It is said, Christmas
comes once a year. But each year
it comes earlier.

In Lent, the days get
longer, sure. But do they shed
any light within?

The season is Lent:
time to prepare for Easter
by adding to faith.

Holy week was once
a time of empty theaters.
Now: a bonanza.

Dust off your Spanish
or your Greek. On Pentecost
we can speak in tongues.

A summer Sunday.
Men forsake twelve apostles
for golf's eighteen holes.

In the fall the leaves
near our small church in Vermont
are colors of God.

Calendar's backward
in the southern hemisphere.
Must be really strange.

BEING ANGLICAN

Anglo-Catholic
walks into a bar and says,
"Just Roman around."

The Oxford Movement.
One starts to expound on it
and eyes glaze over.

Book of Common Prayer
needs a more modern label:
user's manual.

The Church of England,
once the colonial boss,
is now a footnote.

We are a broad church,
have been from the very start.
That's why we have fights.

Anglicans all sing
"Build a new Jerusalem…"
The question is where?

It's good to see that
the House of Bishops knows to
honor July 4th.

Schism seems like such an outdated problem for a modern-day church.

Our tent is so big
that we can even make room
for lapsed governors.

The Church of England's Wilberforce freed the Empire's slaves without a war.

BEING
CHRISTIAN

We launch prayers like darts—for friends, enemies, peace. Maybe some will stick.

It's easier to
pray for your enemies with
your eyes tightly shut.

You want to put your
treasure where your heart is. Where
have you put your heart?

We're evolved people.
Can't we discuss creation
intelligently?

Those ashes on the forehead are embarrassing. You might look Christian.

Peter denied Christ
three times. And you, do you tell
people you know him?

Adult baptism
was once called "Baptism for
those of Riper years."

About St. Paul: Some
of us can't warm up to him.
What are we to do?

Our currency is
doubt. Slowly, we spend it on
faith. Good investment.